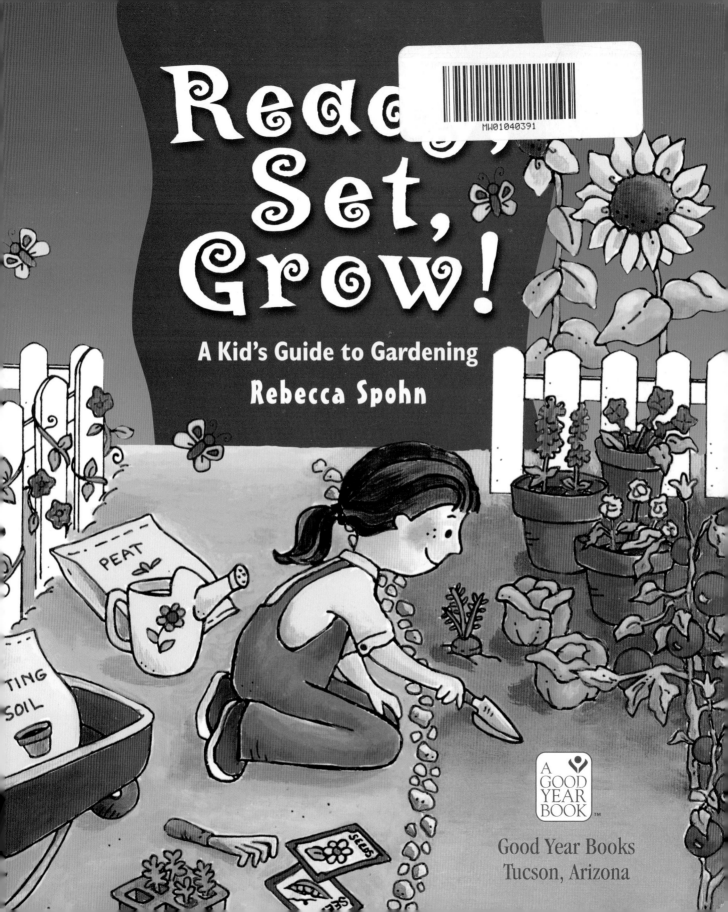

Ready, Set, Grow!

A Kid's Guide to Gardening

Rebecca Spohn

Good Year Books
Tucson, Arizona

GOOD YEAR BOOKS

Our titles are available for most basic curriculum subjects plus many enrichment areas. For information on other Good Year Books and to place orders, contact your local bookseller or educational dealer, or visit our website at www.goodyearbooks.com. For a complete catalog, please contact:

Good Year Books
PO Box 91858
Tucson, AZ 85752-1858
www.goodyearbooks.com

Cover Redesign: Sean O'Neill
Text Redesign: Gary D. Smith, Performance Design
Original Cover and Text Design: Lynne Grenier
Drawings: Rebecca Spohn

Contents

An Introduction for Kids — 1

An Introduction for Adult Helpers — 3

How Does a Seed Grow? — 5

Indoor Gardening

Getting Started — 8

Magic Bean Sprouts — 10

Watching the Grass Grow — 12

Growing an Herb Garden — 14

Carrot Top Plant — 16

Beet Top Plant — 18

Pineapple Plant — 20

Sweet Potato Plant — 22

Avocado Tree Plant — 24

Spider Plant — 26

Boston Fern — 28

English Ivy — 30

Piggyback Plant — 32

Miniature Gardens — 34

Cactus Gardens — 36

Outdoor Gardening

Getting Started 38

    Caring for Your Garden 40

    Transplanting Tips 40

    Weeding 40

    Watering 41

    Garden Visitors 42

    Fences 43

    Pinwheels 44

    Scarecrows 46

    Wiggly Garden Helpers 47

Growing Fruits and Vegetables

    Tomatoes 48

    Radishes 50

    Carrots 52

    Lettuce 54

    Cucumbers 56

    String Beans 58

    Corn 60

    Pumpkins 62

    Gourds 64

    Watermelons 66

Growing Flowers

    Zinnias 68

    Marigolds 70

    Petunias 72

    Snapdragons 74

    Sunflowers 76

    A Strawberry Garden 78

Food and Fun from the Garden

Recipes

    Carrot Cake and Raisins 81

    Glazed Carrots 82

    Garden Salad 83

    Watermelon Fruit Cocktail 84

    Tomato Bowls 85

    Cucumber Boats 86

    Mini-Kabobs 87

    Roasted Pumpkin Seeds 88

    "Little Bits" Vegetable Salad 89

Crafts

    Gourd Maracas 90

    "No-Carve" Jack-o'-Lantern 91

    Seed Paintings 92

AN INTRODUCTION FOR KIDS

Would you like to grow your own pumpkins, shuck your own corn, or make a salad using your own home-grown tomatoes? YOU can!

You can grow all kinds of fruits, vegetables, and flowers, and you can grow them almost anywhere. Whether you live in the country or in the city—whether you have a big backyard or only room enough for a window box—**YOU** can be a gardener!

By following **Ready, Set, Grow!**, you will learn how a seed grows; what tools to use for both indoor and outdoor gardening; how to prepare seedbeds; and, most of all, how to get started!

In this book you will also discover how to recycle all kinds of containers—from milk cartons to paper cups—turning them into miniature gardens.

You will be amazed at how easy it is to grow vegetable-top gardens and water gardens. You will learn how to create a cactus garden, make a terrarium, and keep a garden journal.

Invite your friends to participate in a sunflower-growing contest to see who can grow the tallest sunflower! You can prepare delicious-tasting recipes from your very own home-grown crops. You can even turn a gourd into a musical instrument and create a scary-looking Jack-o'-Lantern without ever carving a pumpkin. Best of all, you will discover how much fun gardening can be.

SAFETY TIPS

- Trying some of the plant activities and recipes in this book may require a little extra help from an adult. If so, you will find an "adult helper" symbol on that page.

- Working with dirt can be fun, but it can also be a "dirty" job, so it is a good idea to wear an old shirt and a pair of jeans.

- When using a shovel to dig in a garden, always wear hard-soled shoes. NEVER jump with both feet onto a shovel. If the soil is too hard, ask an adult to help turn over the soil.

- Be sure to clean your tools with warm water after you use them. Always dry your tools so that any metal will not rust. Carry sharp tools carefully and keep them stored away from a little brother or sister.

- Remember: running with sharp garden tools can be dangerous!

2

AN INTRODUCTION FOR ADULT HELPERS

Ready, Set, Grow! A Kid's Guide to Gardening offers an entertaining and informative way to introduce children to the wonders of gardening. This book is filled with more than 30 "how-to" tips on growing a variety of plants, from creating a carrot-top garden to growing a beanstalk. Easy and fun-to-prepare recipes are also included. These provide children an opportunity to turn the fruits of their labor into tasty and healthful salads and snacks. "Fun from the Garden" offers children further enjoyable and easy activities and crafts using plants that they have grown themselves.

3

Each "planting" page features several sections: "Did You Know?" presents interesting and unusual facts that help build a child's knowledge of science, geography, and history. "Try This" provides additional activities, which are designed to encourage a child to actively participate in learning by doing.

The glossary term on each planting page introduces an important garden-related word. And the reading list offers titles of books about the particular vegetable or fruit being discussed. These books help children read and learn more about a particular plant, vegetable, or fruit.

 Safety is an important part of any activity. Each planting page, craft, or recipe that may require an adult helper is easy for you and a child to identify. Look for the "Adult Helper" symbol through the book. This symbol lets you know that a particular activity may need your watchful eye as you and the child garden together.

HOW DOES A SEED GROW?

When you take a bite of a watermelon, have you ever noticed the black seeds inside, or the seeds in the center of an apple, or the hard seeds in an orange? Have you ever wondered how a seed grows and turns into a plant?

A seed is very much like an egg. Both are filled with protein (food) and a small embryo (in this case, a plant). If the seed is given sunlight, water, air, and lots of care, it will sprout into a seedling.

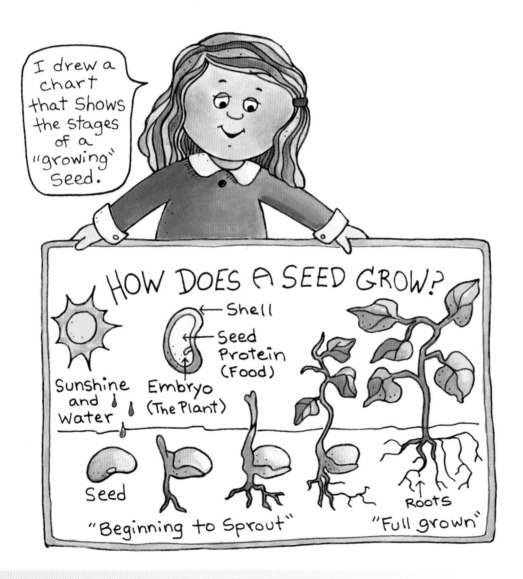

A healthy plant needs food, water, air, and sunlight. Plants get food, or what we call **nutrients**, from rich soil and water. Much like the vitamins and minerals we take to keep us strong and healthy, plants, too, need a daily dose of minerals and nutrients.

Plants use their roots to sip up the nutrients from the water present in the soil. The stem of the plant helps the nutrients travel up to every part of the plant. The sunlight helps the plant mix the nutrients in its green leaves and with a little help from carbon dioxide—which is present in the air—makes energy-building food. This "plant process" has a very long name, **photosynthesis** (FOH to SIN thus sis). Photosynthesis is very important to plants and to us because as the plant makes food, it gives off oxygen, which we need in order to breathe.

HEALTHY PLANTS NEED:

Water: Check the soil around your indoor and outdoor plants each day. If the soil feels dry, give the plants a little drink. But be careful. Too much water will make the soil muddy and may drown your plants.

Sun: Place indoor plants in a sunny spot or on a windowsill. Outdoor plants need the sun's light and warmth, too. Some need more, some less. Remember to read your seed packet to learn when and where to plant your seeds.

Soil: It is important to get the soil ready before you plant seeds or seedlings. Using a rake or trowel, break up any hard clumps of dirt and then rake until smooth. This will help your seedlings when their roots start to grow. Some soil is very sandy or mostly clay and does not contain many nutrients, so a "compost fertilizer" can help provide your plants with food to give an added boost. You can make your own compost with grass clippings and leaves.

SEE FOR YOURSELF:

When you plant seeds in dirt, you miss seeing the seeds begin to sprout and the roots grow. Here is a way to watch.

YOU WILL NEED:

- A clean jar
- Paper towels
- Several large seeds (beans are a good choice)

WHAT TO DO:

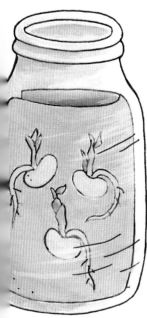

1. Place a paper towel inside the jar so that it presses against the sides.

2. Push 4 or 5 seeds down between the paper towel and the glass.

3. Add a small amount of water, just enough to soak the paper towel.

4. Find a sunny spot for your jar garden. In about a week, your seeds will crack open and send out slender roots.

(Note: It is very difficult to grow houseplants from seeds, so it is best to start with a cutting from another plant. You can either ask an adult to purchase a houseplant for you or you can ask a friend who owns a houseplant to give you a cutting.)

Indoor Gardens

GETTING STARTED
YOU WILL NEED:

- A spoon, fork, or trowel
- Containers
- Newspapers for easy clean-up
- Potting soil recipe: 1 part packaged potting mix, 1 part sand or perlite, 1 part peat moss

WHAT TO DO:

For indoor gardens you will want to make a seedbed. Although a seedbed is not like a real bed that you and I would sleep in, it is a good place to start your seedlings.

First spread newspapers on your work area. Next, be sure to choose the right container. Milk cartons, ice-cream cartons, or coffee cans are all good choices. Place a saucer underneath each container to catch any excess water each time you water the plants. Ask an adult helper to punch holes in the bottom of the container with a hammer and nail.

Now add some pebbles to the bottom for proper drainage. Next you can fill the container with potting soil, about ½ inch from the rim. All plants need soil to grow. You can buy potting soil at nurseries or stores, or you can make your own using the recipe on this page.

8

Once you have planted your seeds, lightly spray the soil with water. It is also a good idea to cover your seedbed with some clear plastic wrap. Place the seedbed in a dimly lit area.

When your seedlings appear, remove the clear wrap. Once your seeds have sprouted, watch that they are not crowding each other. If they do, it may be necessary to transplant the strongest to their own pots.

Remember when caring for your plants, add just enough water so that it runs through the soil and reaches the saucer. If too much water is sitting in the saucer, pour it out. Plants HATE wet feet!

Indoor Gardening

Magic Bean Sprouts

Abracadabra! In just 5 days you can create a jar garden of bean sprouts and eat them in a sandwich or a salad. Actually, the only hocus pocus you will need for this magic trick is a clean quart-size screw-top jar, ½ cup of "mung" beans, which you can find at a grocery or health-food store, and some water.

WHAT TO DO:

Wash beans and let them soak in cold water overnight.

Punch holes in the jar lid.
(Ask an adult helper to use a hammer and nail.)

Drain your beans and put them back in the jar.
This time screw on the lid.

Rinse the beans a couple of times a day.
Be sure to keep the jar in a dark place.

Presto! In 5 days your beans will be ready to eat. They are especially good in a salad or stir-fried in salad oil with other vegetables.

10

DID YOU KNOW?

A kind of bean that grows in Mexico and South America can jump! Well, it may look like magic when it jumps and rolls from side to side. Actually, the larva of a moth lives inside the bean. It can move the bean several inches at a time by holding onto the silk-like wall of the bean with its legs and snapping its body. Americans call these beans "jumping beans." In Mexico, they are "leapers."

TRY THIS!

- Mexico is our neighbor. It borders California, Arizona, New Mexico, and Texas. Find it on a map.
- Mexico, South America, and the American Southwest can be very hot places to live. The people who live there often use the sun as a design in their artwork. You can make a sun picture using a piece of heavy cardboard with glitter. Draw your sun face and rays using a pencil. Fill in your design areas with glue. Then sprinkle different colors of glitter, using one color at a time. Allow your sun picture to dry before hanging, or your glue will run. Your sparkling masterpiece will surely brighten any room.

What did the doctor remove from his salad?

Kidney beans!

GLOSSARY TERM

Larva   The immature stage of many kinds of living things, such as insects, fish, and frogs, is called the *larva*. The best-known larva is the hungry leaf-eating caterpillar that turns into a beautiful butterfly. Another well-known larva is the tadpole, which becomes a bullfrog.

READ ON

Moon Rope/Un lazo a la luna by Lois Ehlert. Harcourt Children's Books, 2003. (Grades K–3)

Mexico ABCs: A Book About the People and Places of Mexico by Sarah Heiman. Capstone Press, 2002. (Preschool–3)

Norma Jean, Jumping Bean by Joanna Cole. Random House, 2003. (Grades K–3)

Mexico! 50 Activities to Experience Mexico Past and Present by Susan Milord. Ideal Publications, 1999. (Grades 3–6)

WATCHING THE
Grass Grow

Don't worry, you will never have to mow this kind of garden. Just have fun watching it grow, grow, grow. All you need is some grass seed, or you can use birdseed, clover, or rye seed, a dish of water, string, and a piece of natural sponge.

WHAT TO DO:

1. Tie the string around the sponge, leaving one long end.

2. Dunk the sponge in water.

3. Sprinkle some seeds onto the sponge.

4. Hang the sponge in a sunny spot.

5. Don't forget to soak the sponge in water at least once a day.

DID YOU KNOW?

There are many, many kinds of grasses: grazing grasses, ornamental grasses, woody grasses (such as bamboo), sugar cane, and cereal grasses. When you eat breakfast, you are really eating grass seeds. Rice, corn, oats, and wheat are in the cereal grass family. People all over the world eat the seeds from these grasses.

TRY THIS!

Take an empty cereal box and turn it into a hand puppet. Cut pieces of construction paper to fit the front, sides, and back of the box. Using glue or a glue stick, secure the paper to the box. Now the fun part is to decorate your "puppet" with crayons, markers, or cut-out construction paper. You can make a lion, clown, robot, monster, or whatever you wish. Then put on a puppet show for others to see.

GLOSSARY TERM

Bamboo   Bamboo is a grass with wood-like stems. It grows very fast and can reach as high as 100 feet tall. The woody stems can be used to make many things, such as bridges, rafts, and houses. Sometimes bamboo is used as a water pipe to carry water to a village.

READ ON

Corn Grows Ripe by Dorothy Rhoads. Troll Communications, 1999. (Grades 4–6)

Wheat by Elaine Landau. Scholastic Library Publishing, 1999. (Grades 3–5)

Pancakes, Pancakes! by Eric Carle. Simon & Schuster Children's Publishing, 2004. (Grades K–2)

Good Bread: A Book of Thanks by Brigitte Weninger. North-South Books, 2003. (Preschool–K)

Heartland: A Prairie Sampler by Jo Bannatyne-Cugnet. Tundra, 2002. (Grades 3–7)

Garden Giggle

Why do worms act so frightened? They have no backbone.

13

GROWING AN
Herb Garden

Thanks to herbs, food like spaghetti sauce, pizza, pickles, and many more taste . . . Grrrrreat! Try planting basil, dill, chives, oregano, parsley, mint, marjoram, thyme, and more.

YOU WILL NEED:

- A small clay flowerpot with a small hole in the bottom
- Potting soil
- Herb seeds
- A shallow pan lined with small pebbles, sand, or vermiculite

WHAT TO DO:

Fill the clay pot with potting soil. Place the seeds in the soil.

Place the clay pot in the pan, and then place the pan in a sunny window.

Water your herb plants by pouring a small amount of water on the pebbles near the bottom of the pot. Also, pour a small amount of water directly on the soil in the pot. Keep both the soil and the pebbles moist, but do not overwater them. The seeds should sprout in 3 to 4 days.

14

DID YOU KNOW?

There are many, many different kinds of herbs. One of these is the fast-growing spearmint. Its heart-shaped leaves are used to flavor iced tea on a hot summer day. The cool mint taste can also be found in candies, toothpaste, and mint jelly. When you chew a stick of spearmint gum, you are chewing the flavor from a spearmint plant.

TRY THIS!

Herbs are easy to dry. You can find herb seeds at most nurseries. Almost any container will make a good home for your herbs. Try a window box, muffin tin, or strawberry pot with pockets.

Once your herb plants bloom, cut about the top ⅓ off the stems. Wash the cut branches in cool water and hang them upside-down in a cool dark spot for a couple of days. Once dry, remove leaves from the stem, and keep them in different jars.

Be sure to cover the jar tightly. Remember to mark each jar so you will know which herb is in it.

GLOSSARY TERM

Vermiculite   This substance is made up of white, inorganic materials that are often used in potting soil to help absorb excess moisture and help the plants "breathe" easier.

READ ON

Kid's Herb Book: For Children of All Ages by Lesley Tierra. Robert D. Reed, Publishers, 2000. (All ages)

From Tree to Table by Susan Ring. Capstone Press, 2003. (Grades K–2)

Garden Giggle

How can you tell that Santa Claus is a wonderful gardener? Because he loves to hoe-hoe-hoe.

Carrot Top Plant

Most everyone loves the taste of garden-fresh carrots and the loud crunchy sound when you take a big bite! Now you can plant your own carrots and enjoy watching the green leafy tops grow.

WHAT TO DO:

First you will need several carrots. Have a parent, or adult helper, cut the tops off as shown:

Save the rest of the carrots for tasty snacking!

Next, place the carrot tops in a shallow bowl filled with gravel and water. Set the bowl on a sunny windowsill. Keep your carrot tops well watered. In 2 to 3 weeks your carrot tops will start to sprout. Soon you will have a feathery, green plant.

16

DID YOU KNOW?

Carrots used to be purple. If you traced the carrot back to its origin in the eastern Mediterranean area in the 1400s, you would find purple carrots. Can you imagine purple carrot sticks in your lunch?

Many years ago in England, ladies decorated their hair with the lacy green leaves of carrots. In early America carrots were orange, but they still didn't look like the carrots we see today. They had very large and coarse roots. These carrots were not often eaten as a vegetable. Instead, they were used as a medicine and as food for livestock.

TRY THIS!

Use paint or crayons to draw a picture in crazy colors. Like the purple carrot, color everything in zany, "unreal" colors—an orange horse in a pink pasture? A purple palm tree on a green beach?

GLOSSARY TERM

Origin   An origin is the very beginning of something. For example, a seed is the origin of a tree.

READ ON

Gathering the Sun: An Alphabet in Spanish and English by Alma Flor Ada. HarperCollins Publishers, 2001. (Preschool–5)

Island in the Soup by Mireille Levert. Groundwood Books, 2001. (Preschool–1)

The Big Carrot: A Maggie and the Ferocious Beast Book by Betty Paraskevas. Simon & Schuster Children's Publishing, 2000. (Preschool–2)

The Carrot Seed by Ruth Krauss. Minnesota Humanities Commission, 2000. (Grades K–3)

Garden Giggle

What is an ant? A hard-working bug that still finds the time to go to lots of picnics.

Beet Top Plant

For an easy-to-grow and colorful plant, try growing a beet top.

WHAT TO DO:

Have an adult helper cut about 2 inches off the top of a beet.

Place the top in a shallow dish filled with gravel and water. Find a sunny spot for your beet top garden.

Remember to keep your garden well watered. Wait and watch, and in no time at all you will have a colorful and fun-looking dish garden!

18

DID YOU KNOW?

The red beet you grow in your garden has a very sweet cousin. This beet, which has white roots, is called a sugar beet. One half of all of the sugar in the United States and much of the sugar in other parts of the world comes from the sugar beet. Sugar is taken from the beet roots by grinding and pressing the roots. Then the juice is boiled and put in vacuum cookers, where sugar crystals are formed.

TRY THIS!

Can you fill in the words that answer the clues below? (Hint: All of the answers rhyme with "beet.")

1. We wear shoes on our __ __ __ __.
2. Fresh fruits and vegetables make a good between-meal __ __ __ __ __.
3. When the sun shines, it provides lots of __ __ __ __.
4. Sugar is __ __ __ __ __.

Answers: feet, treat, heat, sweet

GLOSSARY TERM

Sugar   This food substance is used to sweeten drinks (such as soft drinks, coffee, and tea) and foods (such as cereal and candy bars). Most table sugars look like fine white sand, but sugar also comes in small cubes or in powdered form.

READ ON

Growing Vegetable Soup by Lois Ehlert. Harcourt Brace, 2004. (Preschool–K)

Two Little Gardeners by Margaret Wise Brown. Golden Books, 2006. (Preschool–K)

Just Try It by Christianne C. Jones. Capstone Press, 2005. (Grades K–2)

Garden Giggle

Why do you have to be careful about telling a secret in a cornfield? Because the corn have ears.

19

Pineapple Plant

With a little patience and a very warm spot, you can grow your own beautiful green pineapple plant.

WHAT TO DO:

1. Have an adult helper cut off the top of a pineapple.

2. Let the top dry on its side for 3 to 4 days. Bury the "fruit part," not the leaves, in a bowl of sand. Keep the sand moist.

3. In 2 to 3 months when your plant has taken root, transplant it to a large pot filled with potting soil. Place it in a sunny spot. Water it often, right on the spiky leaves.

Don't be disappointed that your plant probably will never produce a pineapple, because pineapples only grow in tropical climates. Nevertheless, you will have a unique plant to enjoy.

←SAVE

DID YOU KNOW?

The pineapple got its name from its appearance—it looks like a pine cone. The fruit is covered with thick, hard, petal-like tips. These tips are very sharp. In Hawaii, where most pineapples are grown, workers use knives shaped like hooks to cut the fruit from the pineapple plant. The workers wear heavy canvas gloves and clothing to guard against injury.

TRY THIS!

- Look up Hawaii on a map. How many islands make up our 50th state? Get a book about Hawaii from your library and read all about the climate, the volcanoes, the people, and each of the islands.
- Draw a picture of Hawaii using some of the things you learned about in your reading.

GLOSSARY TERM

Canvas A closely woven, coarse cloth made of cotton or linen.

READ ON

Fun with Asian Food: A Kids' Cookbook by Devagi Sanmugam. Tuttle Publishing, 2005. (Grades K–6)

High Tide in Hawaii by Mary Pope Osborne. Random House Books for Young Readers, 2003. (Grades K–3)

A Is for Aloha: A Hawaii Alphabet by U'ilani Goldsberry. Sleeping Bear Press, 2005. (Grades K–5)

Garden Giggle

How do you

make a

pineapple

turnover?

Try tickling

its stomach.

21

Sweet Potato Plant

This kind of plant grows in water instead of soil. All you need is a glass or jar,
a few toothpicks, water, and a sweet potato.

WHAT TO DO:

Fill the glass or jar with water about ⅓ from the top. Poke in four toothpicks evenly spaced around the middle of the sweet potato. The toothpicks will help keep the potato from falling into the water. You want only the tip of the potato in the water. If you see small purple shoots starting to grow at one end, be sure to keep the other end in the water.

Place the glass in a dimly lit area. In about a week the potato will begin to sprout roots, and shortly after that, leaves will appear. Tie strings to a curtain rod or some other high place so your sweet potato leaves can begin to climb.

Remember to change the water often to keep it clean.

22

DID YOU KNOW?

Sweet potatoes originated in Mexico. Over the years, sweet potatoes began to appear in South America and Polynesia. Several varieties of sweet potatoes are common: red, yellow, white, and brown. Today in the South Pacific and Asia, sweet potatoes are an important source of food because the roots are high in vitamins. Many people from villages in New Guinea eat sweet potatoes as their main food.

TRY THIS!

- Make believe you are a detective and explore your backyard. See what you can find, such as a bird's feather, rocks, different kinds of trees and plants, ant hills, weeds, and more.
- Draw a map of your backyard and the places of all of your discoveries.

GLOSSARY TERM

Polynesia   A group of South Pacific islands, including Hawaii, Samoa, Tonga, and others.

READ ON

The Legend of Spud Murphy by Eoin Colfer. Miramax Books, 2005. (Grades 1–5)

Stir, Squirt, Sizzle: A Nick Cookbook by Nickelodeon. Chronicle Books, 2004. (Grades 2–6)

Leon and the Champion Chip by Allen Kurzweil. HarperCollins Children's Books, 2005. (Grades 2–6)

One Potato: A Counting Book of Potato Prints by Diana Pomeroy. Harcourt Children's Books, 2000. (Preschool–1)

Garden Giggle

What most looks like half of a watermelon? The other half.

23

Avocado Tree Plant

An avocado plant can grow to 3 feet or taller—maybe taller than you!

WHAT TO DO:

Save the pit from an avocado. Let it dry for at least 24 hours. Then carefully remove the outer brown skin.

Push 4 toothpicks into the middle of the pit.

Fill a glass with water almost to the top. Place the pit into the glass with the pointy end up. The bottom should rest in the water. Place in a sunny room, but avoid direct sunlight.

In about a week the seed should start to split open and you will see a root grow out of the bottom of the avocado pit.

When you spot the root, transplant your pit into the very middle of a big container filled with soil. Cover the top of the pit with at least 1 inch of dirt.

Move your container to a very sunny spot. Remember to gently turn the pot a little each day so it won't grow toward the light. Water it a little every day. If you are lucky, your small avocado pit will grow into a green leafy tree.

DID YOU KNOW?

The avocado has a funny nickname, "alligator pear." The skin of an avocado is dark green and bumpy, just like the skin of an alligator. The outside of the avocado may not be very pretty, but the inside is smooth and buttery. It has a nutty taste that makes avocado slices perfect for salads. Mashed avocados mixed with other seasonings make a tasty dip for chips or crackers.

TRY THIS!

Make an alligator puppet using a small cereal box. This will be the mouth of your alligator. On the side of the box without perforation marks, cut the box in half, cutting through the top and down both of the skinny sides. Do not cut all the way through the bottom side. Add scary teeth and big eyes with construction paper and glue. You can paint the cereal box with green acrylic paint, if you like.

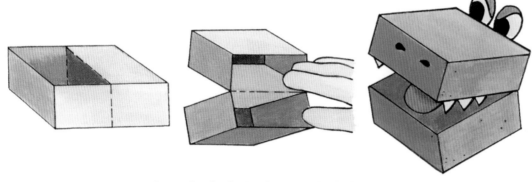

GLOSSARY TERM

Nickname   A nickname is a second name given to a person, place, or thing, often given in fun. A nickname can be a shortened form of a person's name. For example, Katherine might be called Katie for short.

READ ON

Betty Crocker's Cook Book for Boys and Girls by Betty Crocker. John Wiley & Sons, 2003. (Grades 4–6)

Food Fight! by Carol Diggory Shields. Handprint Books, 2002. (Grades K–1)

Look and Cook: A Cookbook for Children by Tina Davis. Stewart, Tabori & Chang, 2004. (Grades K–6)

What kind

of salad

do

snowmen

like to

eat?

Coldslaw.

25

Spider Plant

*Don't let the name of this hanging plant "bug" you. Spider plants only resemble those 8-legged creatures. The main "spider" or "mother" plants grow slender branches called **runners**. At the end of these runners sprout little plants that are spider-shaped. This is why you often see spider plants in hanging baskets.*

W H A T   T O   D O :

Ask an adult to purchase a small spider plant for you, or ask a friend who has a spider plant to give you a small cutting.

As soon as the smaller plants grow roots, you can snip them off of the mother plant and repot them. If possible, you might try potting the baby spider plants before removing them from the mother or main plant by seating the pots next to the main pot. After a few days when you feel the roots of the baby plants have taken hold in their new home, snip them off of the main plant.

Remember to provide your plants with lots of direct light, and water them well once a week. In no time at all, you will find yourself surrounded by green hanging spider plants of all sizes. Share the smaller plants with your friends, or give them as special gifts.

26

DID YOU KNOW?

Although they cannot hear you or feel vibrations, your plants like it when you talk or sing to them. When you do so, you breathe out two things that plants like, carbon dioxide and water. Plants need both of these in order to stay healthy.

TRY THIS!

Find the following words in the puzzle:
Dirt • Green • Plants • Sun • Water

```
R I L J F D L
A C T L O I W
N M K W Y R B
F P L A N T S
G S R T H E U
G R E E N V N
O B A R C D E
```

GLOSSARY TERM

Resemble   If one thing looks like another thing, we say they "resemble" each other. For example, brothers and sisters often resemble each other.

READ ON

Whose Garden Is It? by Mary Ann Hoberman. Harcourt Children's Books, 2004. (Preschool–2)

Diary of a Spider by Doreen Cronin. Joanna Cotler Books, 2005. (Preschool–3)

Feely Bugs by David A. Carter. Simon & Schuster, 2005. (Preschool–2)

Miss Spider's Tea Party by David Kirk. Scholastic, 2006. (Preschool–3)

Garden Giggle

Why would a soldier salute a cornfield? Because of all the kernels (colonels).

Boston Fern

*You don't have to live in Boston, or any city for that matter,
to enjoy this hardy plant.*

WHAT TO DO:

1. As with other houseplants, it is best to start with a cutting or a plant you've purchased from a nursery or supermarket.

2. Ferns love shady humid environments, so be sure to spray your Boston fern's leaves every day with a fine mist of lukewarm water.

3. You may have to give your Boston fern a "haircut" every so often by cutting off any dried or yellowed leaves.

DID YOU KNOW?

Ferns do not have flowers. Without flowers, ferns cannot produce seeds. Instead, ferns reproduce from spores. A mature fern has spores on the underside of its leaves. When these spores grow into little disks, the disks produce male and female cells, which join together to form a new fern plant.

Ferns are very hardy, which means they need little help to grow. They live in moist, shady woods in all parts of the world. Ferns come in many different shapes and sizes. Some ferns in South America grow to be 40 feet tall.

TRY THIS!

Use construction paper and poster paint to make a plant print. Lay a fern flat on a sheet of newsprint. Sponge poster paint on top of the fern. Now carefully lay a sheet of colored construction paper on top. Sandwich the fern between the two sheets. Use your hands to press very hard. Remove the top construction paper. You will have created a pretty print.

GLOSSARY TERM

Hardy   Able to survive rough or difficult conditions, such as cold or drought.

READ ON

Flower Lullaby Book by Takayo Noda. Dial Books for Young Readers, 2006. (Preschool–3)

Spring Is in the Air by Golden Book Staff. Random House Children's Books, 2004. (Preschool–1)

If I Ran the Rain Forest: All About Tropical Rain Forests by Bonnie Worth. Random House Books for Young Readers, 2003. (Grades K–3)

29

English Ivy

This "climbing-vine" houseplant is one of the most popular plants around. Its beautifully shaped, deep-green leaves add color to any room. Filtered sunlight and most cool areas make this ivy very happy. Like ferns, remember to spray the ivy's leaves with a fine mist of water every few days. Keep away from hot, dry spots. Tie strings to a curtain rod or some other high place so your ivy can begin to climb.

DID YOU KNOW?

Ivy plants are very good climbers. Some twist their stems around stronger plants and climb higher and higher. They crawl up walls by growing small roots on their stems. They can cover the outside of an entire building.

Other crawling plants include Virginia creepers, which have little pads that cling to walls as well as other surfaces. Climbing roses use sharp thorns to climb walls and fences.

TRY THIS!

- Make a list of other plants and animals that like to climb.
- Try the fingerplay, "Itsy Bitsy Spider."

The itsy, bitsy spider climbed up the water spout.

Down came the rain and washed the spider out.

Out came the sun and dried up all the rain,

And the itsy, bitsy spider climbed up the spout again!

GLOSSARY TERM

Thorns   Thorns are sharp points on plants, such as roses, which help the plants climb but also serve as protection.

READ ON

Creeping Vine by Felicia Law. Capstone Press, 2005. (Grades K–3)

Extraordinary Rain Forest by Scholastic Inc. Staff. Scholastic, 2003. (Grades 1–4)

Morning Glory by Sandra Comino. Groundwood Books, 2006. (Grades 1–5)

Garden Giggle

What

flower

is like

a crazy

pickle?

A

"daffy"

dill.

Piggyback Plant

*The piggyback plant has clusters of hairy, heart-shaped leaves called **plantlets**, which seem to ride piggyback on larger leaves. Piggyback plants love partial sun and spring-like temperatures.*

WHAT TO DO:

1. If you want to start new piggyback plants, simply cut a plantlet from an existing plant and place it in sand. (Do not use ocean sand.)

2. In no time at all, roots will sprout. Once this happens, repot new plants in small containers.

3. Keep your plants well-watered.

32

DID YOU KNOW?

Each kind of plant has its own kind of "feet," or roots. Some roots burrow down, some spread out just under the surface of the soil, but all of them do the same job—keeping plants standing straight and tall and absorbing water and minerals from the soil. When you transplant a plant, be careful to dig enough soil around the plant so you won't cut the roots by mistake.

TRY THIS!

Can you unscramble the "underground" words below?

```
R   M   O   W
T   A   W   E   R
E   E   S   S   D
R   T   S   O   O
D   S   H   A   R   I
R   R   S   O   T   A   C
E   O   S   A   O   T   T   P
```

Answers: worm, water, seeds, roots, radish, carrots, potatoes

GLOSSARY TERM

Absorb   To soak up or to drink in liquids. For example, a sponge is able to absorb large amounts of water.

READ ON

Rain Forest by Fiona MacDonald. Scholastic Library Publishing, 2000. (Grades 2–5)

Plants by Margaret Whalley. T & N Children's Publishing, 2004. (Grades 3–5)

Plant Book by Pamela Hickman. Kids Can Press, 2000. (Grades 1–5)

Why are fruits so polite? They always remember to say, "Thank you 'berry' much!"

33

MINIATURE GARDENS

*Plants that love moist and humid conditions will love living in a garden inside a jar or glass. These gardens are called **terrariums** or **dish gardens**. When making a terrarium, you can choose from a number of plants. Below is a list of a few. Think about the shape, height, look, and color of each plant when deciding what to include in your terrarium.*

Aluminum Plant
Unlike a pop can, the aluminum plant is not made of aluminum. It only looks that way because of its green and silver-colored leaves. These plants can grow to more than 9 inches high.

Artillery Plant
This plant gets its name from its ability to release little clouds of pollen "like a shot." With its tiny leaves, this plant makes a nice border in a terrarium or dish garden. A warm, moist place is best for its good health.

Chinese Evergreen
If you searched the floor of an Asian jungle, you might find a Chinese evergreen. These plants love moist and shaded areas. They will, however, grow in almost any condition. These striped plants can also be planted in pots of their own.

Prayer Plant
This plant is called a prayer plant because at night its leaves fold upward like clasped hands. When the day comes, its leaves unfold. These brown-spotted and green leaves enjoy moist, humid environments, so this plant will be a fun addition to your terrarium. Make sure your prayer plant receives only filtered light.

Snake Plant
The snake plant is an absolute for any terrarium. This tall, striped plant grows best in dim light. And because its leaves store water, the snake plant needs very little.

YOU WILL NEED:

- A clean glass container, jar, or even a fish bowl
- Plastic wrap and a rubber band or string to make a lid
- Pebbles or aquarium gravel
- Bits of charcoal
- Potting soil
- Long-handled spoon
- A spray bottle
- Bent coat hanger for placing plants in the terrarium
- Four or five plants

WHAT TO DO:

1. Start by laying in a thin layer of pebbles or gravel. Add a thin layer of charcoal and about 2 to 3 inches of soil. **SAFETY TIP:** Remember, when using a glass container, never force your hand into a small opening. The glass could break.

2. Next, decide which plants you want to place in your terrarium and how you want to arrange them.

3. Make holes for your plants using the spoon. Lower your plants into the holes with the bent coat hanger.

4. Pat the soil around each plant with the spoon. Use the spray bottle to moisten the soil. Add twigs, rocks, or small toys for decoration.

5. Finally, stretch the plastic wrap over the opening of the container and fasten with a rubber band or string.

Place your terrarium in a brightly lit spot, but not in direct sunlight. If the glass begins to fog up in your jar, making it hard to see inside, simply remove the cover for several hours. At other times, if your soil looks dry, spray it with a little water.

What dangerous green things should you jump away from? A thundering herd of pickles.

Cactus Gardens

Bring a little of the Southwest into your home by creating an unusual and interesting cactus dish garden. There are many different varieties of cactus that come in different colors and shapes.

What sets a cactus apart from most plants is its ability to store water. Like a camel, a cactus can live long periods without water. It's a good practice, then, to only water your dish garden once or twice a month.

WHAT TO DO:

First choose a shallow container, maybe a low, wide clay pot. You might even want to decorate your pot with southwestern-looking designs. To give you some ideas, go to your library for books on Native American rugs and pottery.

Pour a layer of pebbles on the bottom of your container. This helps drainage. Then add a layer of charcoal bits.

Now you're ready to place your cactus. Place these small pots in the dish filled with pebbles and charcoal.
SAFETY TIP: Watch out! A cactus has sharp prickly needles. If you don't have thick garden gloves, use a folded newspaper to pick up your cactus plants.

Place your dish garden in a very sunny spot. For a final touch, add small rocks or toys to create a special desert scene!

36

DID YOU KNOW?

Cacti can survive a long time without water. Unlike other plants that lose water through their leaves, a cactus is made up of thick stems and has no leaves. These stems can store water inside them. The sharp spines on the cactus stop thirsty animals from getting to its water storage. With such special features, a large cactus can live for two or more years without additional water.

TRY THIS!

- Arizona, our 48th state, is home to many different kinds of cacti. Cacti have the hot temperatures of a desert, but they aren't the only desert dwellers. Many kinds of birds and animals have also learned to adapt to the often harsh conditions of the desert. Visit your public library and read about the desert.
- Look in a book about desert animals and birds and find the road runner. Draw a picture of one using crayons and markers.

Garden Giggle

What could be called "nature's pincushion"? A cactus.

GLOSSARY TERM

Cacti   This is the plural of the word *cactus*, meaning "more than one cactus."

READ ON

The Sonoran Desert by Day & Night by Dot Barlowe. Dover Publications, 2003. (Preschool–3)

Around One Cactus: Owls, Bats & Leaping Rats by Anthony D. Fredericks. Dawn Publications, 2004. (Preschool–5)

The Great Southwest Activity Book by Rising Moon. Northland Publishing, 2004. (Grades K–5)

37

Outdoor Gardens

GETTING STARTED

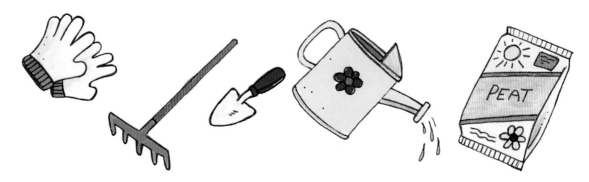

YOU WILL NEED:

- Gardening gloves
- A garden rake, shovel, hoe, trowel, watering can, or hose
- A sunny garden patch
- Natural fertilizer

An outdoor gardener knows two things: First, it's important to wait for warm weather before starting an outdoor garden, and second, it's important to use the right tools for each job. For this one, you will need a garden rake to smooth the surface of the soil and remove any lumps or bumps; a shovel to dig large holes for transplanting plants; a hoe for digging up weeds; garden gloves for handling fertilized soil; and a trowel to dig little holes for seeds.

Be on the lookout for the perfect garden spot. Search your yard for a spot that is sunny and has rich soil. This is soil that contains little sand and clay. It's easier to start out with a small garden, so you might want to plan one that is really two small gardens, each 6 feet by 6 feet, with a foot in between for a path.

Prepare the soil by breaking up the dirt with a hoe or garden rake. This is also a good time to add some natural fertilizer, which an adult can purchase for you at a nursery or supermarket. Use a hoe or rake to work the fertilizer into the soil.

SAFETY TIP: Be sure to wear gloves when working with fertilizers.

The best part of growing a garden is deciding what to grow in it. Just as an artist paints a picture, the choice of what color to use and where to place it on a canvas can be a challenge, but a lot of fun, too! Begin by thinking about how much room each plant will need (if it's a vine plant, it will need room to spread), how tall each plant will grow, and what colors and shapes you want in your garden. It's a good idea to keep taller plants such as cornstalks and sunflowers toward the back of your garden; climbing and vine plants like peas, tomatoes, watermelons, and pumpkins toward the outer sides of your garden; short and root crops such as radishes, onions, and lettuce in the middle; and low flowers like zinnias, marigolds, and snapdragons in the front to add a dash of color.

CARING FOR YOUR GARDEN

TRANSPLANTING TIPS

Sometimes you will want to move a potted indoor plant to your outdoor garden. To do so, follow these steps:

1. Be sure all danger of frost has passed.
2. Set out your plants for a few days before planting them. This will help them get used to outdoor living.
3. Scoop out as much soil around your plants as possible before replanting them in your garden.
4. Dig roomy holes in your garden. Roots don't like cramped quarters.
5. Always give new transplants a good watering.

WEEDING

Your garden will not be a healthy, happy garden if the soil is too dry or is overgrown with unwanted plants. Weeding and watering are very important. Weeds are simply plants that grow where you do not want them. Weeds are thieves—they will steal food and water from the plants you do want.

40

If your plants are still seedlings, it will be hard to tell what is a weed and what is not. So when you first plant your seeds, try to keep them in straight rows and use garden markers to identify what you planted in each row.

Grab weeds at the bottom of the stem and pull straight up. Be sure to get the roots, or the weed will grow back. Weed regularly. If you are having a hard time with weeds, don't worry. You can still win the battle by using mulch, which is like putting a blanket on the unwanted weeds. Mulch helps keep sunlight from reaching the soil so weeds can't grow. It also seals in moisture, keeping the soil moist and soft. You can use store-bought mulch or leaves, straw, or wood chips.

Once you have weeded around your seedlings, spread the mulch all around, about 2 or 3 inches deep. Remember not to cover any of your plants.

WATERING

Before watering any plant, check the soil first. If it feels damp, wait and water when the soil is dried. To water potted plants, use a watering can or a garden hose with a spray nozzle and water only once every 5 to 7 days. Set the nozzle for a fairly gentle spray. In addition, shiny-leaved plants love to have their leaves misted with water. (Never mist fuzzy-leaved plants.) A plastic spray bottle works fine.

You may need to water your garden every morning if it receives lots of sun throughout the day. Only water enough to moisten the soil. Too much water and you will have a puddle of mud—your plants could drown.

GARDEN VISITORS

When you watch old westerns, it's easy to tell the "Good Guys" from the "Bad Guys." But it's not always so easy to tell good and bad insects apart. The good news is that all garden visitors aren't bad. Some of the Good Guys include earthworms, spiders, ladybugs, honeybees, and birds. Many of these garden visitors eat bad insects or help to pollinate flowers! Meanwhile, you need to know the Bad Guys to keep your garden healthy.

First, pretend you are a detective. Use a magnifying glass to check the leaves and stems of your plants. If you find holes and it appears that some leaves have been chewed in half, or some have curled edges, you definitely have some uninvited guests in your garden. Some of these bad pests may be aphids, caterpillars, earwigs, snails, slugs, or white flies. Garden pests can suck juices from your plants or eat the leaves and stems. This could kill your plants.

To rid your garden of unwanted bugs, try using a spray bottle filled with soapy water. Bugs hate the taste of soap and it won't damage your plants. For earwig problems, set some damp newspapers in the middle of your garden overnight. By morning, your newspaper will have attracted lots of earwigs. Throw them away in a garbage bag.

Keeping pests away may be a daily job, but the rewards of having a healthy garden are well worth it!

FENCES

Use a fence to keep hungry rabbits and other animals from entering your garden. You can purchase a decorative garden fence, or some gardeners prefer plain chicken wire. You can even make your own!

WHAT TO DO:

1. Use stakes about 24 inches high. Stick stakes into the ground every 36 inches. Go around your entire garden.
2. Using strong, heavy string, wrap string around each stake, from one stake to another. Go around and around your garden with the string, moving up the stakes every 2 inches. Keep the string taut.

Your new fence should help protect all of your hard gardening work.

43

PINWHEELS

Pinwheels can be a colorful and fun accent in your garden. Pinwheels spinning in a summer breeze are a pretty sight to see. Try making pinwheels yourself.

YOU WILL NEED:

- Heavy manila paper
- Crayons
- Pencil with eraser top
- Straight pin
- Scissors
- Pattern

WHAT TO DO:

1. Trace and transfer the pattern onto the manila paper.

2. Decorate your pinwheel with crayons.

3. From each corner, cut halfway to the center, about 2½ inches.

4. Next, fold every other corner of the paper toward the center.

5. Ask an adult to help you push a straight pin through the center and into the pencil's eraser.

Make as many as you like. Place them in or around your garden to discourage rabbits and other unwelcome visitors.

SCARECROWS

A scarecrow may or may not scare away every crow, but they are a fun addition to your garden.

YOU WILL NEED:

- Shirt, pants, gloves, and hat
- 1 plain pillowcase
- 1 permanent marker
- Heavy string

- Straw
- 2 strong sticks, one 4 feet long and the other 6 feet long
- Hammer and nails

WHAT TO DO:

1. Lay the 4-foot stick across the 6-foot stick about 12 inches from the top, making a t-shape.

2. Ask an adult to hammer nails into the two pieces to keep them together.

3. Pound the t-frame into the ground about one foot. If the soil is too hard, soften it by watering.

4. Draw a funny face near the top of the pillowcase. Fill the top half with straw and pull it over the top of the 6-foot stick. Tie it on tightly with string.

5. Fill the pants, shirt, and gloves with straw. Remember to tie string around the openings so the straw won't fall out.

6. Ask an adult to attach the clothes to the sticks using safety pins or nails. For an added touch, try dressing up your scarecrow with a funny hat or sunglasses.

WIGGLY GARDEN HELPERS

What could be better for your garden than growing helpers who will do much of the work that needs to be done underneath the soil? As worms wriggle through the ground, they loosen the dirt, allowing air and water to more readily reach your plants' roots.

WHAT TO DO:

1. First, find a large box and fill it with soil, about 2 inches from the top. You may want to line your box with a garbage bag so the dirt won't spill through the cracks.

2. Mix into the soil tiny pieces of leaves, dead plants, or scraps from the kitchen to make the soil good for the worms. Then spray the soil until moist.

3. Carefully find 5 or 6 worms and place them in the worm box. Cover your box with a cardboard lid. Make sure to punch air holes in the lid! Keep the box in a cool, shady place and keep the soil moist.

In no time at all, check to see how many new worms have been produced. Remove a few every so often and introduce them into your garden. Remember, keep your wriggly worm box moist and full of nutrients, such as pieces of leaves.

Tomatoes

Instead of a trip to the supermarket, you can now enjoy a trip to your garden. A garden can be like having a mini-supermarket right in your own backyard. And home-grown vegetables and fruits are sure to taste better.

There's nothing quite like the juicy taste of a ripe red tomato bursting in your mouth. Tomatoes are fun to grow because there are so many different varieties from which to choose. Start your tomatoes in a seedbed (see page 8) in your house about 4 weeks before the last frost. Then, follow these steps.

WHAT TO DO:

When your seedlings are about 6 inches tall, find a sunny spot outdoors. Plant your seedlings approximately 2 feet apart.

Because tomato plants are vine plants, when your plant is 12 inches tall, provide a stake for it. As the tomato grows, tie the stems loosely to the stakes.

Keep the soil around your tomatoes moist. Depending on the variety of tomatoes you choose, most will be ready to pick in 8 to 10 weeks.

48

DID YOU KNOW?

A tomato is really a fruit, but because it is used in soups, sauces, and ketchup for main meals, it is often thought of as a vegetable. In fact, in 1893 the Supreme Court declared it a vegetable. And can you guess which country grows more tomatoes than any other nation? The answer is the United States.

TRY THIS!

Thanks to many early explorers, we enjoy foods that are not native to the United States but have become long-time favorites.

In your library, look for a cookbook with recipes from around the world. Invite a friend to dinner and serve dishes from a particular country, such as China, Italy, or Poland. If the friend invites you to his or her house, the next dinner could include foods from a different country.

Garden Giggle

Why was the tomato blushing? Because it saw the salad dressing.

GLOSSARY TERM

Seedbed   A bed of soil where seedlings are grown.

READ ON

I Will Never Not Ever Eat a Tomato by Lauren Child. Candlewick Press, 2003. (Preschool–2)

Pizza Pat By Rita Golden Gelman. Random House Children's Books, 1999. (Grades K–1)

Pizza at Sally's by Monica Wellington. Penguin Young Readers Group, 2006. (Preschool–1)

49

Radishes

No summer salad would be complete without the hot feisty taste of a ripe radish. And radishes are the fastest-growing vegetable in town!

W H A T   T O   D O :

1. Plant your seeds about ⅛ inch deep with about 3 to 4 inches in-between.

2. Seedlings will sprout in as little as a week.

3. Water and weed your plants, and your radishes should be ready to pick in only 4 weeks.

DID YOU KNOW?

We usually think of radishes as being small, red, and round. But did you know that some radishes are called "icicles" because they are long and white? Whatever color they are, all radishes are a tasty source of Vitamin C.

TRY THIS!

Can you unscramble these picnic favorites? Match the unscrambled food with its picture.

R C R T A S O
S E I D R A H S
P L S E A P
N C R O

Answers: carrots, radishes, apples, corn

GLOSSARY TERM

Icicle   A pointed, hanging piece of ice formed by dripping water that later freezes.

READ ON

Bumpety Bump! by Pat Hutchins. HarperCollins Children's Books, 2006. (Preschool–2)

Little Gardener's Activity Book by Fran Newman-D'Amico. Dover Publications, 2005. (Preschool–2)

Rosey Rabbit's Radish: Letter R by Scholastic Press. Scholastic, 2001. (Preschool–1)

What fruit is not afraid to take a swim?

A watermelon.

51

Carrots

These crunchy orange vegetables are called "root plants." When they are ready to harvest 65 to 70 days after planting, you'll find them growing downward under the ground like a root.

WHAT TO DO:

Soak your carrot seeds in water overnight.

Plant the seeds ⅛ inch deep and about 1 to 2 inches apart. Cover them firmly with soil.

Water lightly every day. In about 2 to 3 weeks your seeds will sprout.

In about a month, thin your plants to about 4 inches between each one. (The tiny carrot that you pull out can make a good snack. Just wash and nibble.)

In 10 to 12 weeks, or when you can see the top of the carrot peeking out of the ground, your carrots should be ready for harvesting.

52

DID YOU KNOW?

Seeds vary greatly in size and shape. Carrots grow from very tiny seeds. There are about 24,000 tiny carrot seeds in just one ounce.

TRY THIS!

- Pack a picnic lunch. If you and your family usually eat inside at a table, break tradition. On a clear, sunny day, it is fun to eat outside, al fresco style. Any kind of sandwich tastes better with a snack of carrot sticks. Pack chips, cheese, and fruit as well.
- Planting gardens brings summer to mind. Summer is also the best time for cloud watching. Have fun stretched out in your backyard watching clouds pass overhead. Try to make mental pictures out of the clouds' shapes. Cumulus clouds are big, puffy clouds, sometimes called "cauliflower" because of their resemblance to the vegetable.

GLOSSARY TERM

Al fresco   This Italian phrase means "in the open air." It is often used to mean "outdoors."

READ ON

In the Garden: Who's Been Here?
by Lindsay Barrett George. Greenwillow Books, 2006. (Grades K–2)

Junior and Laura Share the Year Together
by Lisa Vischer. Zonderkidz, 2003. (Preschool–K)

Fruits and Vegetables/Frutas y Vegetales
by Gladys Rosa-Mendoza. Me+mi Publishing, 2002. (Preschool–1)

Garden Giggle

There is

only one

way to

raise a

carrot right.

Grab hold

of the

top of it

and pull.

53

Lettuce

Rabbits like to nibble lettuce, so you might want to protect your garden from these hungry, woodland friends with a chicken-wire fence around your garden.
(See "Fences" on page 43.)

WHAT TO DO:

1. Be sure to choose a very sunny spot in your garden. Lettuce loves full sun.

2. Plant seeds about 1½ to 3 inches apart and only ⅛ inch deep. Too deep, and your seeds won't sprout.

3. Water gently!

4. When your seedlings reach 3 to 4 inches high, thin by pulling out every other one.

In about 2 months your lettuce leaves will be ready to eat. Pick the outside leaves from the lettuce head so it will continue to grow. Always wash garden foods before eating. Remember, if 2 heads are better than 1, then 3, 4, or more are even better. So plant as much lettuce as you want for cool, crispy salads.

54

DID YOU KNOW?

When you plant a seed, do you know if it is upside-down or not? You may not, but the seed does. In the growing tip of each seed are tiny granules. These react to gravity and help tell the seed which way to grow. No matter which way you plant the seed, it will always send its roots down and its shoots up.

TRY THIS!

Draw a topsy-turvy upside-down world. Imagine an Earth where you could walk on your bedroom walls and stand on the ceiling. What would you see?

GLOSSARY TERM

Gravity   A force that draws all things toward the center of the Earth. Gravity is what keeps us from falling off the Earth!

READ ON

Tomato, Lettuce and Wriggly Worms! by Diana James. T & N Children's Publishing, 2004. (Grades K–3)

Wishing Star by Moira Butterfield. Barron's Educational Series, 2002. (Preschool–K)

Force Makes Things Move by Kimberly Brubaker Bradley. HarperCollins Children's Books, 2005. (Grades K–4)

Garden Giggle

How do you make friends with a squirrel? Climb a tree and act like a nut.

Cucumbers

In about six weeks these green, bumpy vegetables will be ready to eat!

WHAT TO DO:

1 Find a warm, sunny spot for your cucumbers to grow. Plant cucumber seeds in small mounds of earth, about 5 to 6 seeds per mound. Be sure there is at least 3 feet between mounds. Cucumbers really spread, so provide lots of room.

2 In about 8 to 10 days, seedlings should appear. Allow at least 2 more weeks to pass before you thin your seedlings.

3 Keep the soil moist but try to keep the leaves on your cucumber plants dry to prevent mildew.

4 In roughly 2 months your cucumbers should be about 6 to 8 inches long and ready to be picked.

DID YOU KNOW?

Vegetables belong to families just as we do. For example, the cucumber belongs to the gourd family. Its relatives include melons, squash, and pumpkins.

TRY THIS!

Fill in the blanks below. For example: A pickle was once a cucumber.

1. A raisin was once a

_____ .

2. A butterfly was once a

_____ .

3. A frog was once a

_____ .

4. A cat was once a

_____ .

Answers:
grape, caterpillar,
tadpole, kitten

WE ARE FAMILY

GLOSSARY TERM

Gourd   This fruit is related to the pumpkin, squash, and melon family. But this is not a fruit you eat; it is an ornamental fruit.

READ ON

Carla's Sandwich by Debbie Herman. Flashlight Press, 2004. (Preschool–3)

Cool as a Cucumber by Sally Smallwood. Zero to Ten, 2005. (Preschool–2)

The Kitchen Talks by Shirley Mozelle. Holt, Henry Books for Young Readers, 2006. (Preschool–3)

Garden Giggle

What is green, bumpy, and can leap tall buildings? Super pickle!

57

String Beans

You probably won't grow a beanstalk as tall as Jack's or climb to a giant's castle, but you can grow fresh garden beans that snap with flavor. Beans can be eaten cooked or right off the vine.

Decide how many rows of beans you would like. It is a good idea to have at least a foot between rows. Beans need plenty of room to grow.

WHAT TO DO:

Plant your bean seeds about 6 inches apart and ½ inch deep.

In about 2 weeks when your seeds have sprouted, thin by pulling out every other seedling, leaving 12 inches in between.

Now is a good time to carefully place a tall stake on either side of your bean patch or row and to tie several rows of string to the stake. This will give your beanstalks something to lean on as they grow.

After about 2½ months, your string beans will flower, and soon after small bean pods will appear where the flowers were. They are ready to pick when the pods are about 3 to 4 inches long. Hold the vine while you carefully pick off a bean pod.

DID YOU KNOW?

Native Americans first introduced string beans to the colonists. These early beans were very stringy and not as tasty as beans are today. They were either "snapped" and boiled for eating or they were left on the vine to grow to maturity. String beans left on the vine will grow big enough to produce hard-shelled beans inside. Once the string bean pods have dried, you can open them to find more beans inside.

TRY THIS!

Count the number of beans in this basket:

Garden Giggle

Which tree is like a pet? A dogwood.

GLOSSARY TERM

Maturity   A state in which a person, animal, or plant becomes full-grown.

READ ON

Jack and the Bean Stalk by Staff of Jump at the Sun. Hyperion Books for Children, 2004. (Preschool–1)

Mud Soup by Judith Head. Random House Books for Young Readers, 2003. (Grades K–3)

Beans to Chocolate by Inez Snyder. Children's Press, 2003. (Grades K–1)

Corn

They say corn can grow as high as an elephant's eye, so watch out.
These tall green and yellow stalks can reach 8 feet tall so be sure to leave plenty of room in your garden.

WHAT TO DO:

1. Start by planting seeds 2 inches deep with about 1 yard between rows. In a little over a week, you should see seedlings sprout. Thin to 12 inches apart.

2. Water well!

3. In about 10 to 12 weeks, your corn should be ready to harvest. Keep a close eye on each ear of corn. If not picked when ready, corn can spoil in a few days. Pull back the leaves and check the kernels. They should be plump and a nice yellow color. Poke a kernel with a fork. If a milky white juice squirts out, it's ready to pick!

60

DID YOU KNOW?

Indian corn, also called *maize*, has red, blue, and black kernels. More than 300 years ago, Native Americans gave the Pilgrims corn to eat so they could survive their first cold winter in America. The very next year, the Pilgrims shared corn that they had grown with the Native Americans to show thanks. That was the first Thanksgiving feast.

GLOSSARY TERM

Maize   *Maize* is a Native American name for this grain. The word for grain in England was *corn*, so the Pilgrims named this grain "Indian corn."

TRY THIS!

Make a crunchy corn treat for birds. Ask an adult to make a bowl of popcorn. Carefully string the popcorn in a long garland using a plastic sewing needle and strong thread. Hang the garland from the branches of a tree in your yard. In no time at all, you will have a flock of feathered friends.

READ ON

The Mystery of the Stolen Corn Popper by David A. Adler. Penguin Young Readers Group, 2004. (Grades 3–5)

I Like Corn by Robin Pickering. Scholastic Library Publishing, 2000. (Grades K–2)

The Lucky Grain of Corn by Veronique Tadjo. Milet Publishing, 2002. (All ages)

Harvest Time by Jennifer Waters. Capstone Press, 2002. (Preschool–2)

Garden Giggle

How can you tell when a farmer is mean? He pulls all the ears off the corn.

Pumpkins

Pumpkin vines spread in every direction, so give them lots of space to roam.

WHAT TO DO:

Begin by planting seeds 1½ inches deep and about 1 yard apart. If you have a large garden, plant rows of pumpkins, keeping 6 feet between rows.

Water and weed the seeds. In about 3 to 4 months, your pumpkins should turn a deep orange and be ready for harvesting.

When the vines begin to die, your pumpkins are ready to pick. Enjoy roasted pumpkin seeds or pumpkin pie.

←— 1 YARD —→

DID YOU KNOW?

Pumpkins can be used for more than Jack-o'-Lanterns and pumpkin pie. They can also be used in recipes for muffins, bread, pudding, and custard. Can you guess how many pumpkins are usually sold in the United States every October? The answer is more than 35 million pounds of pumpkins.

TRY THIS!

- Ripe pumpkins, cool winds, and colored leaves mean fall is in the air. This is a good time of year to make a harvest doll. Using cornhusks, wrap a husk over a cotton ball and tie it with string to make a neck. Use another husk for the upper body and tie it at the waist. Add arms by pulling some husk through the inside of the upper body. Tie string at the wrists. Let the rest of the husk fall from the upper body part. This will create a skirt (to create pants, pull the husk apart and tie it at the ankles of the doll).

- Decorate yourself as a Jack-o'-Lantern for Halloween by creating a papier-mâché mask. Cover one side of an inflated balloon with narrow strips of newspaper and papier-mâché. Coat with several layers. Once dry, pop the balloon with a pin. Decorate your mask with acrylic paints. Add feathers or beads, if you like. Glue and tape a large tongue depressor to the inside of the mask to use as a handle.

What does a witch use to fix a flat tire? A pump-kin.

GLOSSARY TERM

Custard   A pudding-like mixture of eggs, milk, sugar, and flavoring.

READ ON

One Child, One Seed: A South African Counting Book by Kathryn Cave. Holt, Henry Books for Young Readers, 2003. (Preschool–2)

From Seed to Pumpkin by Wendy Pfeffer. HarperCollins Publishers, 2004. (Preschool–K)

The Pumpkin Book by Gail Gibbons. Holiday House, 2000. (Grades K–3)

Gourds

Gourds are funny looking, and because of their crazy shapes and colorful patterns, you're sure to find them fun to grow. Gourds are great to use for all kinds of things, such as decorations, bird houses, and lamp bases.

WHAT TO DO:

As soon as the danger of frost has passed, start by planting your gourd seeds in a sunny spot, about ½ inch deep.

Once the gourd seeds have sprouted, thin them out, leaving about 10 to 12 inches between plants.

Provide a tall stake, fence, or trellis on which the gourds can climb. The vines produce beautiful leaves as well as the crazy-looking gourds.

In about 10 to 12 weeks, your gourds should be ready for picking. Keep your gourds in a dry, cool place until they dry out.

DID YOU KNOW?

People living in what is now known as Mexico were growing gourds more than 8,000 years ago. One of these gourds, the luffa, was used as a washcloth for bathing. The inside of the dried gourd is full of fibers that make a bath cloth or sponge.

TRY THIS!

- Decorate a gourd with scratch designs. Once the gourd has dried thoroughly, cover it with a black crayon. Try to press hard so you cover the gourd completely. Using a nail or pin, carefully scratch designs into the crayon layer.
- You can turn your gourd into an animal depending on its shape. For example, if you want it to be a bird, draw feathers in the crayon layer.

Garden Giggle

What can

you use

to keep

spaghetti

from falling

off your

plate?

Tomato paste.

GLOSSARY TERM

Fibers   Threadlike structures that combine one with another to form animal or vegetable tissue.

READ ON

My Great Grandmother's Gourd by Cristina Kessler. Orchard Books, 2000. (Grades K–4)

Pumpkin Decorating by Vicki L. Rhodes. Sterling Publishing Company, 2002. (Preschool–3)

Pumpkinhead by Eric Rohmann. Random House Children's Books, 2003. (Grades K–4)

65

Watermelons

"Melon, melon, who's got the melon?" You will, when you follow a few basic "watermelon-growing" rules.

WHAT TO DO:

First, make sure the threat of frost has passed. When you are ready to plant, make mounds of soil, 1½ feet wide. Leave 5 feet between each mound. Using your hand, flatten the top of the mound.

Next, turn the mound into an island by scooping out a ditch around the mound. Watermelons love warm, moist soil, so fill the circular ditch to the top with water. Space 4 seeds in the mound about 1 inch deep.

In a few days your watermelon seedlings will sprout, but it will take all summer for them to grow into watermelons. You'll know when your watermelons are ripe by checking the curly tendrils near the stem. Once ripe, the tendrils will have turned from green to brown.

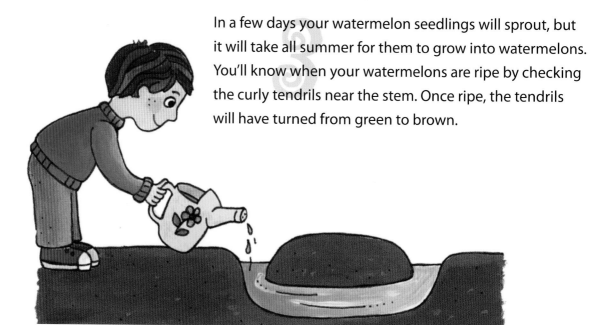

DID YOU KNOW?

The watermelon originated in Africa. Pumpkins came to America in 1620, when the Pilgrims brought watermelon seeds with them. Within ten years, watermelons were growing all over Massachusetts. The Native Americans liked watermelon so much that they began planting them. Because the seeds were so easy to carry and plant, soon watermelons were growing in all parts of North America.

TRY THIS!

Unscramble the following names of fruits and match them to their pictures.

AWTRELOMEN   _____

RNGOAE   _____

PARE   _____

RSTABWERYR   _____

PLPAE   _____

Answers: watermelon, orange, pear, strawberry, apple

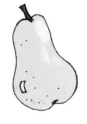    

GLOSSARY TERM

Continent   A continent is a large body of land surrounded by water. There are seven continents on Earth: Africa, Antarctica, Asia, Australia, Europe, North America, and South America.

READ ON

The Berenstain Bears and the Missing Watermelon Money by Stan Berenstain. Random House Books for Young Readers, 2001. (Grades K–3)

Summer: An Alphabet Acrostic by Steven Schnur. Houghton Mifflin Company, 2001. (Grades K–3)

Tiny Hands: Summer by Anna Galera Bassachs. Barron's Educational Series, 1999. (Preschool–1)

Why does

a rabbit

have a

shiny nose?

Because its

powder puff

is at the

other end.

Zinnias

Zinnias are vibrant, perky flowers that prefer lots of sunlight and warmth. When in full bloom, zinnias are as colorful as a box of crayons.

WHAT TO DO:

They are very easy to grow from seed. Simply scatter the seeds onto the soil and rake them into the surface. Keep the soil well watered, and in a few days seeds will sprout. In 6 weeks your zinnias will be in full bloom. Remember, they love lots of sunshine!

DID YOU KNOW?

Almost 400 years ago, the colonists brought to America what the Native Americans called "the white man's fly"— the honeybee. Today we can thank the honeybee for producing tasty honey and for helping pollinate plants.

TRY THIS!

Have fun with your friends by trying to create as many different words as possible from the word "honeybee." Good luck!

GLOSSARY TERM

Pollinate   A process in which bees transfer pollen from one part of a flower to another, allowing the flower to reproduce.

READ ON

Friendly Flowers by Golden Books. Golden Books, 2003. (Grades K–2)

Waiting for Wings by Lois Ehlert. Harcourt Children's Books, 2001. (Grades K–2)

A Walk in the Woods Coloring Book by Dot Barlowe. Dover Publications, 2003. (Preschool–3)

So Happy! by Kevin Henkes. HarperCollins Publishers, 2005. (Preschool–3)

Garden Giggle

Do you think flowers will grow in my hair? Why should they? I've been watering the roots!

69

Marigolds

Marigolds are especially fun and easy to grow. These bright orange, red-orange, or yellow flowers are very hardy plants. The most important ingredient for their good health is lots and lots of sunshine.

*Some marigolds only grow 6 to 7 inches high. These are called **dwarfs**. Others can grow up to 2 to 3 feet tall. Be sure to read the information provided on the back of the seed packet to find out which type you have.*

WHAT TO DO:

Start your marigolds in a seed bed around mid-April. In no time at all, your seeds will have sprouted.

You can either transplant your seedlings outside after any danger of frost has passed, or you may put the strongest in individual pots. If transplanting outdoors, space the seedlings about 12 to 15 inches apart. They will bush out as they grow. Of course, you can also plant them in your garden from seed when the weather becomes warm enough.

Because marigolds are annual flowers, you will have to reseed them each year. So when the blossoms close, pull them off and save the seeds.

70

DID YOU KNOW?

Bugs will turn and run if they see marigolds in your garden. The flowers' pungent peppery odor chases bugs away. Other friends of your garden are birds, which eat harmful insects, such as corn borers. Skunks are also good for your garden, because they eat crickets, beetles, and grasshoppers.

TRY THIS!

Collecting seeds from flowers is fun and saves you money. Once you have grown your own flowers, you don't have to buy flower seeds again. As soon as most flowers stop blooming, they often "go to seed." This means that the bloom has dried and begins to form seeds. Follow these steps to gather your seeds:

1. Place a clear plastic bag over a blossom that has gone to seed. Tie it securely.
2. To save the remaining plant, cut off the blossom with the bag still attached.
3. Lightly shake the bag and the seeds will begin to fall into the bag.
4. Remove the seeds by carefully opening the bag and pouring them into an envelope. Place each variety of flower seeds in individual envelopes. Remember to write the name of the flower on each envelope.
5. Save your seeds in a place that is dry and not too hot.

GLOSSARY TERM

Corn Borers   These insects are the larva of a moth that feeds on corn and other plants.

READ ON

Plantzilla by Jerdine Nolen. Harcourt Children's Books, 2005. (Grades K–3)

The Stars Will Still Shine by Cynthia Rylant. HarperCollins Children's Books, 2005. (Preschool–3)

Why was the pickle-o (piccolo) player asked to leave the orchestra? Because all he could play were sour notes.

71

Petunias

Petunias bloom in a variety of pretty colors, such as purple, red, pink, white, blue, and more. Petunias are strong hardy flowers and, depending on the variety, can grow from a few inches to almost 2 feet. To grow petunias:

WHAT TO DO:

Begin by choosing a very sunny spot.

Plant seeds 12 inches apart. Be sure to water well. In no time at all, your petunias will grow and provide blooming color.

DID YOU KNOW?

Each of the states in the United States has a state flower. In 1891 New York was the first state to choose a state flower. New York schoolchildren voted for the rose as their state's emblem.

TRY THIS!

- Go to your library and look up your state's flower. Find out what that flower needs to grow, and plant it in your garden, if possible.

- Make flower puppets from two paper plates. Start by cutting one paper plate in half. This will be the back of your puppet. Now staple the plates together. Cut out petals from different colors of construction paper and staple or glue around the edges of the front plate. Add a funny flower face with markers.

GLOSSARY TERM

Emblem   An emblem is a symbol of an idea. It can also be a symbol of things for a person or country. For example, the American flag is an emblem of the United States.

READ ON

Petunia by Roger Duvoisin. Knopf Publishing Group, 2000. (Preschool–3)

Color Your Own Flower Seed Packet Illustrations by Marty Noble. Dover Publications, 2004. (All ages)

Why did the boy take a carrot to bed? To feed his nightmare.

Snapdragons

If you are wondering how a flower can get such a ferocious name, just take a look at these blossoms. Try pinching the sides of a snapdragon blossom. You will quickly discover that the blossom opens and shuts just like a dragon's mouth.

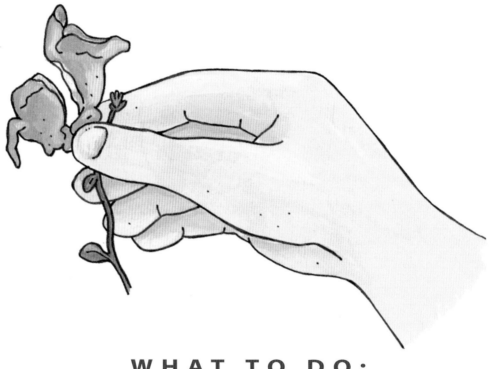

WHAT TO DO:

1. You can start with seeds or seedlings after the danger of frost has passed. Snapdragons can grow from 1 to 3 feet tall!

2. These seeds are small, so cover them just barely with soil.

3. Keep the soil moist. Snapdragons enjoy plenty of sun and will bloom in a variety of bright colors from early in the growing season to late summer.

74

DID YOU KNOW?

People have used perfumes since the beginning of recorded history. They have been found in 3,000-year-old Egyptian tombs. By the 1500s, perfumes were used and enjoyed all over Europe.

When you smell lovely sweet perfumes or soaps, you are really smelling flowers. That is because most perfumes are made from flowers and plants. The fragrance is taken from plants in several ways. The first way is by passing steam through the petal, turning the sweet oil from the flower into a gas. The gas is forced through a tube and then cooled into a liquid once more. The second way is to boil the flower petals in water instead of using steam.

TRY THIS!

When you visit your local library, look for books on where products come from. Find out how paper is made from trees, how spearmint gum is made from an herb, or how art paints are made.

GLOSSARY TERM

Fragrance   A sweet, pleasant odor.

READ ON

The Animal Garden by Michelle Angers. Publish America, 2004. (All ages)

The Fairest Scents of All by Andrea Posner-Sanchez. Random House, 2005. (Preschool–1)

The Orange Trees of Versailles by Annie Pietri. Random House Children's Books, 2005. (Grades 3–5)

Garden Giggle

How can you tell when a chef is mean? When he beats the eggs and whips the cream.

75

Sunflowers

These fast-growing flowers will add a bright yellow color to your outdoor garden!

WHAT TO DO:

In early May plant seeds about ½ inch deep and 2 to 3 feet apart in a sunny patch of your garden.

Water well.

Your sunflowers will sprout in about 2 weeks.

76

DID YOU KNOW?

Artists throughout time have used flowers in their paintings. One of the most famous flower paintings is called *Sunflowers* by Vincent Van Gogh. He lived in the 1800s in the Netherlands and southern France. He painted several different sunflower pictures and colored each one a bit differently.

TRY THIS!

Once your sunflowers are fully grown, try painting a picture of them.

What vegetable looks like it was in a fight? A black-eyed pea.

GLOSSARY TERM

Netherlands   A country in Western Europe. Its capital is Amsterdam.

READ ON

Sunflower Houses: Inspiration from the Garden by Sharon Lovejoy. Workman Publishing Company, 2001. (Grades 3–6)

This Is the Sunflower by Lola M. Schaefer. Greenwillow Books, 2000. (Preschool–1)

77

A Strawberry Garden

Like pumpkins, you can grow a strawberry patch or, easier yet, a "Strawberry Pot." This kind of pot has pockets to hold individual plants. You can purchase a pocket pot from a local nursery. To create a strawberry pot, start in early spring by buying June-bearing or "Everbearing" strawberry plants. Your strawberry plant will produce strawberries all summer long if you start with "Everbearing" plants.

WHAT TO DO:

Put gravel on the bottom of the pot. Add rich soil. Tuck a plant in each pocket and keep them well watered. Be careful not to bury the "crown." This is the swollen part of the plant that divides the top, where the leaves come from, and the roots. The crown should be at ground level or your plants might rot.

Provide lots of sun for your strawberry pot garden. When the strawberries are red from top to bottom, they are ready to pick and enjoy. Rinse them in cold water, and use them to top a bowl of cereal or vanilla ice cream.

The first year your plant will produce small, sweet-tasting berries. The following year— an even BIGGER crop! Don't forget . . . when cold weather arrives, be sure to protect your strawberry pot garden with a plastic covering. This will help your plants survive the winter.

DID YOU KNOW?

The tiny fruit fly plays one of the most important roles in laboratories around the world. Because it reproduces so quickly, a scientist can study 30 generations of fruit flies in a single year. It would take 500 years to study 30 generations of humans!

TRY THIS!

Try to find your way through the strawberry patch to the bowl of strawberries and cream.

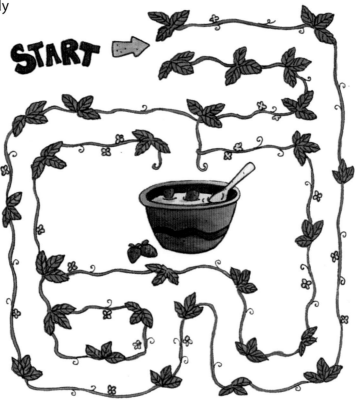

START ➡

Knock,

Knock!

Who's there?

Berry!

Berry who?

Berry nice

to meet you!

GLOSSARY TERM

Fruit Fly   A fly whose young feed on fruits and vegetables.

READ ON

First Strawberries: A Cherokee Story retold by Joseph Bruchac. Penguin Young Readers Group, 1998. (Preschool–3)

Good Humor Man by Kathleen N. Daly. Golden Books, 2001. (Preschool–1)

Batterup Kids: Delicious Desserts Sweet Treats from the Premier Children's Cooking School by Barbara Beery. Gibbs Smith, 2004. (Grades K–6)

FOOD AND FUN FROM THE GARDEN

Carrot Cake and Raisins

By following this easy recipe, you can "stir-up" a delicious dessert using a favorite vegetable.

YOU WILL NEED:

1½ cups grated carrots

1⅓ cups water

1½ cups brown sugar

1 cup raisins

1 tsp. cinnamon

2 tsp. butter

2 tsp. baking soda

2 cups whole wheat flour

½ tsp. salt

WHAT TO DO:

1. Ask an adult to help you cook the carrots, sugar, raisins, and water in a saucepan.
2. Boil 7 to 8 minutes.
3. When tender, add butter and cinnamon
4. Next, add dry ingredients to mixture.
5. Ask an adult to bake in a loaf tin or 9-inch square pan at 375° for 45 minutes.

81

Glazed Carrots

This recipe is easy and tasty. Glazed carrots are sometimes called "golden coins," because they are shiny and have a golden color.

YOU WILL NEED:

5 to 6 carrots
½ tsp. salt

2 tbsp. brown sugar
2 tbsp. butter

WHAT TO DO:

1. Wash the carrots in cold water. Ask an adult to cut the carrots into thin slices.
2. Cook carrots in a small amount of water for about 15 minutes, or until tender.
3. Drain the carrots and add butter, brown sugar, and salt.
4. Simmer over low heat until the carrots look shiny. Remove from heat, and serve.

Garden Salad

This yummy side dish is truly "garden-grown"!

YOU WILL NEED:

½ head of lettuce
1 tomato, sliced

½ green onion
Several radishes and cucumbers, sliced

WHAT TO DO:

1. Be sure to wash the lettuce and tomato thoroughly.
2. Tear lettuce pieces into a salad bowl.
3. Add the tomato, onion, radishes, and cucumbers.
4. Top with your favorite salad dressing and lightly stir or toss. You may enjoy other garden greens in your salad, such as fresh, uncooked peas or green beans.

83

Watermelon Fruit Cocktail

YOU WILL NEED:

1 can of fruit cocktail
1 watermelon

Butter knife
Mixing bowl and spoon

WHAT TO DO:

1. Ask an adult to cut the watermelon into slices.
2. Now you can carefully take a butter knife to cut bite-sized pieces of watermelon from the 1-inch slices.
3. Mix with the fruit cocktail.
4. Chill for at least an hour.
5. Serve as a cool fruit dessert.

84

Tomato Bowls

This recipe is both fun to eat and fun to look at.

YOU WILL NEED:

1 large tomato

Your favorite sandwich spread

A few lettuce leaves

1 hard-boiled egg

WHAT TO DO:

1. Begin by washing the tomato and lettuce. Blot lettuce leaves and arrange them on a dish.
2. Position the tomato on a cutting board with the top facing up. Ask an adult to cut out the stem of the tomato. Next, cut the tomato into quarters, but not all the way through.
3. Gently pull the tomato sections apart.
4. Fill the tomato with your favorite spread.
5. Peel the hard-boiled egg and cut into slices. On the lettuce leaves, arrange the egg slices around the stuffed tomato. You have created a dish fit for a king!

Cucumber Boats

What is green, has a sail, and carries a yummy cargo?
A "cucumber boat"!

YOU WILL NEED:

1 cucumber

Sandwich or cheese spread

1 slice of whole wheat bread

Vegetable peeler

Knife

Toothpicks

WHAT TO DO:

1. Ask an adult to remove the skin of the cucumber with a vegetable peeler.
2. Ask an adult to slice the cucumber in half the long way.
3. Now, using a spoon, scoop the seeds out of the center of the cucumber halves.
4. Fill the cucumber centers with your favorite spread or tuna fish salad.
5. Remove the crust from a slice of bread. Cut it diagonally to form two triangles. Using toothpicks, stand the bread triangles up in the middle of the cucumber boat. These will be the sails.
6. Serve.

Mini-Kabobs

These are fun to make and to eat! Share them with your friends.

YOU WILL NEED:

6 1-inch cubes of ham
Cherry tomatoes
Cucumbers

Radishes
Cheese
Toothpicks

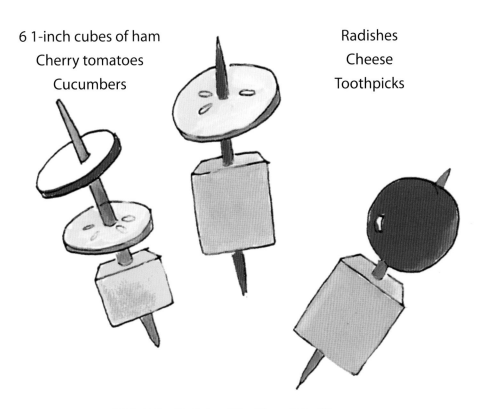

WHAT TO DO:

1. Ask an adult to cut the meat and vegetables into bite-sized pieces.
2. Next put the meat and vegetables in any order on individual toothpicks.
3. If you want, dip your kabob into a favorite salad dressing.

Roasted Pumpkin Seeds

When Halloween is here, it is always fun to create your own scary or funny-looking Jack-o'-Lantern. But remember not to overlook the great-tasting snack you can make out of leftover pumpkin seeds.

YOU WILL NEED:

1 pumpkin
Spoon
Paper towels

Salt
Wax paper
Cookie sheet

WHAT TO DO:

1. Ask an adult to preheat the oven to 350°.
2. Save the scooped-out seeds on waxed paper. Wash the seeds under cold water and blot dry between paper towels.
3. Spread out seeds on a cookie sheet. Sprinkle with salt.
4. Roast seeds for 30 minutes to 1 hour.

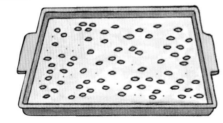

"Little Bits" Vegetable Salad

This salad is truly "mixed-up" with good-tasting, bite-sized vegetables and delicious dip.

YOU WILL NEED:

Lettuce

Carrots

Radishes

Cucumbers

Tomatoes

Sour cream or yogurt

Mixing bowl and spoon

WHAT TO DO:

1. Ask an adult to cut the vegetables into small, bite-sized pieces.
2. Mix all of the vegetables together with sour cream or yogurt in a mixing bowl.
3. Serve on a plate of lettuce.

89

Gourd Maracas

A maraca is a musical instrument. To make some of your own, you will need two gourds and an adult helper.

WHAT TO DO:

1. Ask an adult to poke a nail hole in each end of a gourd. This will help dry out the inside of the gourds.
2. When the gourds are completely dry, the seeds will become loose. It's fun to shake the gourds to a beat and hear the sounds they produce.
3. With acrylic paints, paint designs or funny faces on your gourds. They will last longer if you shellac them. If you see signs that they are spoiling, throw them away. You can always grow more.

"No-Carve" Jack-o'-Lantern

As leaves begin to fall and colder winds begin to blow, it's time to prepare for that "trick-or-treat" holiday . . . Halloween! This means it's time to turn your very own home-grown pumpkins into funny or fearsome-looking Jack-o'-Lanterns.

WHAT TO DO:

1. Many people carve pumpkins with a knife, but for an easier and safer way, try painting. You can use permanent markers or acrylic paints. Begin by using a ball-point pen to sketch out the Jack-o'-Lantern's features.
2. Color with paints or markers.
3. Display your Jack-o'-Lantern on a table. Have a "spooktacular" time!

Seed Paintings

You will need a variety of seeds in different shapes, sizes, and colors to create your seed mosaic. For example, you may want to create an underwater scene with a big fish.

WHAT TO DO:

1. First draw the outline of your own design onto a stiff piece of cardboard. Using your finger, spread a thin layer of white glue onto a small area of your picture.

2. Next, have fun placing your seeds onto the glued areas. Keep the seeds close together. You may want to shellac your final artwork to give the seeds some shine and luster. And you can even frame the finished piece!